Overcoming
Life's Greatest
CHALLENGES

APPLYING GOD'S TIMELESS
TEN COMMANDMENTS *to the*
STRUGGLES *of* TODAY

PAUL CHAPPELL

Striving Together Publications
4020 E. Lancaster Blvd.
Lancaster, CA 93535
800.201.7748

Cover design by Andrew Jones
Layout by Sarah Michael and Craig Parker
Edited by Monica Bass
Special thanks to our proofreaders.

ISBN 978-1-59894-078-7

Printed in the United States of America

Table of Contents

THE TEN COMMANDMENTS

1   *Thou shalt have no other gods before me.*

2   *Thou shalt not make unto thee any graven image.*

3   *Thou shalt not take the name of the LORD thy God in vain.*

4   *Remember the sabbath day, to keep it holy.*

5   *Honour thy father and thy mother.*

6   *Thou shalt not kill.*

7   *Thou shalt not commit adultery.*

8   *Thou shalt not steal.*

9   *Thou shalt not bear false witness against thy neighbour.*

10   *Thou shalt not covet thy neighbour's house.*

Keeping God First

Text

EXODUS 20:2–3
2   I am the LORD thy God, which have brought thee out of the land of Egypt, out of the house of bondage.
3   Thou shalt have no other gods before me.

Overview

God has just brought the Israelites out of Egypt where they had lived in slavery for four hundred years and had been influenced by the polytheism of Egyptian worship. He brings them to a mountain in the desert to reintroduce Himself and claim first place in their worship as the only true God.

Lesson Theme

God desires to build an intimate relationship with us based on His unconditional love and grace. Growth can only occur in this relationship when we put Him first in our lives, worshipping Him for who He is, not for who we want Him to be.

Introduction

_____

_____

_____

I. The _Identification_ of Our God

A. The _Name_ of God

EXODUS 3:13–14

13 And Moses said unto God, Behold, when I come unto the children of Israel, and shall say unto them, The God of your fathers hath sent me unto you; and they shall say to me, What is his name? what shall I say unto them?

14 And God said unto Moses, I AM THAT I AM: and he said, Thus shalt thou say unto the children of Israel, I AM hath sent me unto you.

B. The _Nature_ of God

II. The _Intervention_ of Our God

A. An intervention of _deliverance_

EXODUS 3:7–8

7 And the LORD said, I have surely seen the affliction of my people which are in Egypt, and have heard their cry by reason of their taskmasters; for I know their sorrows;

8 And I am come down to deliver them out of the hand of the Egyptians, and to bring them up out of that land unto a good land and a large, unto a land flowing with milk and honey; unto the place of the Canaanites, and the Hittites, and the Amorites, and the Perizzites, and the Hivites, and the Jebusites.

B. An intervention of grace

III. The Indication **of Our God**

A. To loyal adoration

ISAIAH 42:8
8 I am the LORD: that is my name: and my glory will I not give to another, neither my praise to graven images.

B. To loving affection

EXODUS 20:5
5 Thou shalt not bow down thyself to them, nor serve them: for I the LORD thy God am a jealous God...

JOHN 15:12
12 This is my commandment, That ye love one another, as I have loved you.

DEUTERONOMY 7:7–8
7 The LORD did not set his love upon you, nor choose you, because ye were more in number than any people; for ye were the fewest of all people:
8 But because the LORD loved you...

1 JOHN 4:10
10   Herein is love, not that we loved God, but that he loved us, and sent his Son to be the propitiation for our sins.

Conclusion

_____

_____

_____

Study Questions

1. Why did God have to remind the Israelites who He was?

2. What circumstances did God remind the Israelites of when He gave them the Ten Commandments?

3. What picture does God reveal to us in delivering the Israelites from Egyptian bondage?

4. What is the foundation of all spiritual freedom?

5. What had the Israelites done to merit God's favor? How does this truth relate to salvation and God's continued work in our lives?

6. What are some attributes of a spiritual polygamist?

7.   How can you cultivate affection for God?

8.   On what do you spend your time, energy, and money?

Memory Verse

ISAIAH 42:8

8   I am the LORD: that is my name: and my glory will I not give to another, neither my praise to graven images.

Keeping Our Worship Pure

Text

EXODUS 20:4–5

4   *Thou shalt not make unto thee any graven image, or any likeness of any thing that is in heaven above, or that is in the earth beneath, or that is in the water under the earth:*

5   *Thou shalt not bow down thyself to them, nor serve them: for I the LORD thy God am a jealous God, visiting the iniquity of the fathers upon the children unto the third and fourth generation of them that hate me;*

1 JOHN 5:21

21   *Little children, keep yourselves from idols.*

Overview

As God is giving the second commandment to Moses on Mount Sinai, Aaron is leading the people in idolatry below. This scenario reveals the depravity of man. Something within the human heart continually attempts to replace God with substitutes. The second commandment gives us the key to keeping our worship pure.

Lesson Theme

The worship God desires from His people is worship that is given in spirit and in truth. Rather than redefining God to fit our lifestyles or attempting to manipulate God to meet our perceived needs, we must consider the demand of the second commandment—that we worship God for who He is. Pure worship is the greatest joy of the Christian life.

Introduction

_____

_____

_____

Exodus 32:1–4

1   And when the people saw that Moses delayed to come down out of the mount, the people gathered themselves together unto Aaron, and said unto him, Up, make us gods, which shall go before us; for as for this Moses, the man that brought us up out of the land of Egypt, we wot not what is become of him.

2   And Aaron said unto them, Break off the golden earrings, which are in the ears of your wives, of your sons, and of your daughters, and bring them unto me.

3   And all the people brake off the golden earrings which were in their ears, and brought them unto Aaron.

4   And he received them at their hand, and fashioned it with a graving tool, after he had made it a molten calf: and they said, These be thy gods, O Israel, which brought thee up out of the land of Egypt.

Exodus 32:7–10

7   And the LORD said unto Moses, Go, get thee down; for thy people, which thou broughtest out of the land of Egypt, have corrupted themselves:

8   They have turned aside quickly out of the way which I commanded them: they have made them a molten calf, and have worshipped it, and have sacrificed thereunto, and said, These be thy gods, O Israel, which have brought thee up out of the land of Egypt.

9   And the LORD said unto Moses, I have seen this people, and, behold, it is a stiffnecked people:

10 Now therefore let me alone, that my wrath may wax hot against them, and that I may consume them: and I will make of thee a great nation.

JOHN 4:24
24 God is a Spirit: and they that worship him must worship him in spirit and in truth.

I. We Must _Worship_ God As He Is

LEVITICUS 19:4
4   Turn ye not unto idols, nor make to yourselves molten gods: I am the LORD your God.

JOHN 4:24
24 God is a Spirit: and they that worship him must worship him in spirit and in truth.

JOHN 1:18
18 No man hath seen God at any time; the only begotten Son, which is in the bosom of the Father, he hath declared him.

A. _Honour_ Him above all others.

DEUTERONOMY 4:15–20
15 Take ye therefore good heed unto yourselves; for ye saw no manner of similitude on the day that the LORD spake unto you in Horeb out of the midst of the fire:
16   Lest ye corrupt yourselves, and make you a graven image, the similitude of any figure, the likeness of male or female,

17 The likeness of any beast that is on the earth, the likeness of any winged fowl that flieth in the air,

18 The likeness of any thing that creepeth on the ground, the likeness of any fish that is in the waters beneath the earth:

19 And lest thou lift up thine eyes unto heaven, and when thou seest the sun, and the moon, and the stars, even all the host of heaven, shouldest be driven to worship them, and serve them, which the LORD thy God hath divided unto all nations under the whole heaven.

20 But the LORD hath taken you, and brought you forth out of the iron furnace, even out of Egypt, to be unto him a people of inheritance, as ye are this day.

B. __Worship__ ***Him above all others.***

II. We Must Not __Use__ God for What We __Want__

DANIEL 3:17–18

17 If it be so, our God whom we serve is able to deliver us from the burning fiery furnace, and he will deliver us out of thine hand, O king.

18 But if not, be it known unto thee, O king, that we will not serve thy gods, nor worship the golden image which thou hast set up.

A. ***We must pray in His*** __name__.

1. His __name__ is authoritative.

JOHN 16:23
23 And in that day ye shall ask me nothing. Verily, verily, I say unto you, Whatsoever ye shall ask the Father in my name, he will give it you.

2. His __will__ is sovereign.

JOHN 15:7
7 If ye abide in me, and my words abide in you, ye shall ask what ye will, and it shall be done unto you.

MATTHEW 6:10
10 Thy kingdom come. Thy will be done in earth, as it is in heaven.

3. His __ministry__ is to mediate.

1 TIMOTHY 2:5–6
5 For there is one God, and one mediator between God and men, the man Christ Jesus;
6 Who gave himself a ransom for all, to be testified in due time.

ROMANS 5:8–10
8 But God commendeth his love toward us, in that, while we were yet sinners, Christ died for us.
9 Much more then, being now justified by his blood, we shall be saved from wrath through him.
*10 For if, when we were enemies, we were reconciled to God **by the death of his Son**, much more, being reconciled, we shall be saved by his life.*

B. *We must pray for His* __will__ .

III. We Must Not __Replace__ God with __Idols__

A. *Idolatry is* __replacing__ *God.*

2 TIMOTHY 3:1–2

1   This know also, that in the last days perilous times shall come.

2   For **men shall be lovers of their own selves,** covetous, boasters, proud, blasphemers, disobedient to parents, unthankful, unholy,

B. *Idolatry is* _____ *against God.*

COLOSSIANS 1:14–15

14   In whom we have redemption through his blood, even the forgiveness of sins:

15   Who is the image of the invisible God, the firstborn of every creature:

ACTS 4:12

12   Neither is there salvation in any other: for there is none other name under heaven given among men, whereby we must be saved.

JOHN 14:6

6   Jesus saith unto him, I am the way, the truth, and the life: no man cometh unto the Father, but by me.

HEBREWS 1:1–3

1 God, who at sundry times and in divers manners [at different times in different ways] *spake in time past unto the fathers by the prophets,*

2 Hath in these last days spoken unto us by his Son, whom he hath appointed heir of all things, by whom also he made the worlds;

3 Who being the brightness of his glory, and **the express image of his person**, *and upholding all things by the word of his power, when he had by himself purged our sins, sat down on the right hand of the Majesty on high;*

Conclusion

1 JOHN 5:21

21 Little children, keep yourselves from idols. Amen.

———————————————————————
———————————————————————
———————————————————————

Study Questions

1.   What were the Israelites doing while God was giving the Ten Commandments to Moses?

2.   Why did God forbid artists' representations of Himself?

3.   What is meant by the statement, "We don't worship what should be used, and we don't use what should be worshipped"? Give an example of how this truth applies to your daily walk.

4.   How could idolatry keep a person from trusting Christ as Saviour?

5.   What are some indications that you are manipulating God rather than worshipping God?

6.   Besides physical idols, what is put in the place of God?

7.   How can you recognize the idols in your life?

8.   What steps will you take to replace the idols with the pure worship of God?

Memory Verses

JOHN 4:24
24 God is a Spirit: and they that worship him must worship him in spirit and in truth.

Keeping His Name Sacred

Text

EXODUS 20:7
7 Thou shalt not take the name of the LORD thy God in vain; for the LORD will not hold him guiltless that taketh his name in vain.

ACTS 4:12
12 Neither is there salvation in any other: for there is none other name under heaven given among men, whereby we must be saved.

Overview

God's name is above every other name—high and lifted up. It is to be feared and reverenced. There are laws to protect our names from slander, but what about God's name? In the third commandment, God gives us a charge to protect His name.

Lesson Theme

As Christians, we have been given the unique privilege and responsibility of keeping God's name sacred. We are to exalt God's name by protecting it from harm and proclaiming it to the world.

Introduction

_____

_____

_____

EXODUS 20:7
7 Thou shalt not take the name of the LORD thy God in vain; for the LORD will not hold him guiltless that taketh his name in vain.

I.   The _Preeminence_ of God's Name

PSALMS 148:13
13 Let them praise the name of the LORD: for his name alone is excellent; his glory is above the earth and heaven.

A. *His name is* _Holy_ .

MATTHEW 6:9
9 After this manner therefore pray ye: Our Father which art in heaven, Hallowed be thy name.

B. *His name is* _highly exalted_ .

GENESIS 1:1
1 In the beginning God created the heaven and the earth.

PSALM 139:7–10
7 Whither shall I go from thy spirit? or whither shall I flee from thy presence?

8   If I ascend up into heaven, thou art there: if I make my bed in hell, behold, thou art there.
9   If I take the wings of the morning, and dwell in the uttermost parts of the sea;
10   Even there shall thy hand lead me, and thy right hand shall hold me.

II. The Protection of God's Name

A. From denial

MARK 3:22
22   And the scribes which came down from Jerusalem said, He hath Beelzebub, and by the prince of the devils casteth he out devils.

MATTHEW 12:31
31   Wherefore I say unto you, All manner of sin and blasphemy shall be forgiven unto men: but the blasphemy against the Holy Ghost shall not be forgiven unto men.

MARK 3:28–29
28   Verily I say unto you, All sins shall be forgiven unto the sons of men, and blasphemies wherewith soever they shall blaspheme:
29   But he that shall blaspheme against the Holy Ghost hath never forgiveness, but is in danger of eternal damnation:

EXODUS 20:7
7   Thou shalt not take the name of the Lord thy God in vain; for the LORD will not hold him guiltless that taketh his name in vain.

EXODUS 20:11

11 For in six days the LORD made heaven and earth, the sea, and all that in them is, and rested the seventh day…

B. *From* deception

2 TIMOTHY 3:12

12 Yea, and all that will live godly in Christ Jesus shall suffer persecution.
13 But evil men and seducers shall wax worse and worse, deceiving, and being deceived.

C. *From* distortion

MATTHEW 7:21–23

21 Not every one that saith unto me, Lord, Lord, shall enter into the kingdom of heaven; but he that doeth the will of my Father which is in heaven.
22 Many will say to me in that day, Lord, Lord, have we not prophesied in thy name? and in thy name have cast out devils? and in thy name done many wonderful works?
23 And then will I profess unto them, I never knew you: depart from me, ye that work iniquity.

D. *From* desecration

EXODUS 20:7

7 Thou shalt not take the name of the LORD thy God in vain…

1. **When His name is used to** _Swear_

LUKE 6:45
45 A good man out of the good treasure of his heart bringeth forth that which is good; and an evil man out of the evil treasure of his heart bringeth forth that which is evil: for of the abundance of the heart his mouth speaketh.

2. **When His name is used for an** _excuse_

MATTHEW 12:34
34 O generation of vipers, how can ye, being evil, speak good things? for out of the abundance of the heart the mouth speaketh.

III. The _Proclomation_ of God's Name

A. *Through our* _testimony_

ACTS 11:26
26 And when he had found him, he brought him unto Antioch. And it came to pass, that a whole year they assembled themselves with the church, and taught much people. **And the disciples were called Christians first in Antioch.**

1 PETER 2:12
12 Having your conversation honest among the Gentiles: that, whereas they speak against you as evildoers, they may by your good works, which they shall behold, glorify God in the day of visitation.

B. *Through our* witnessing

ACTS 8:4

4   *Therefore they that were scattered abroad went every where preaching the word.*

Conclusion

PHILIPPIANS 2:9

9   *Wherefore God also hath highly exalted him, and given him a name which is above every name:*

10   *That at the name of Jesus every knee should bow, of things in heaven, and things in earth, and things under the earth;*

11   *And that every tongue should confess that Jesus Christ is Lord, to the glory of God the Father.*

ACTS 4:12

12   *Neither is there salvation in any other: for there is none other name under heaven given among men, whereby we must be saved.*

_____

_____

_____

Study Questions

1. What do the Bible names of God reveal to us?

2. What is blasphemy, and how do people blaspheme the Holy Spirit?

3. Why must we be careful about believing a person who says, "God told me to tell you"?

4. What does swearing indicate about a person?

5. Is there anything in your life (actions, habits, possessions, attitudes, speech, etc.) that is harming God's name?

6. What steps will you take this week to grow in your love for God so that you will be more alert to protecting His name?

7. How can you respond when those around you take the Lord's name in vain?

8. How are you proclaiming the name of Christ to the lost, or how will you begin?

Memory Verses

PHILIPPIANS 2:10–11

10   That at the name of Jesus every knee should bow, of things in heaven, and things in earth, and things under the earth;
11   And that every tongue should confess that Jesus Christ is Lord, to the glory of God the Father.

Keeping His Sabbath Rest

Text

EXODUS 20:8–11

8   *Remember the sabbath day, to keep it holy.*

9   *Six days shalt thou labour, and do all thy work:*

10   *But the seventh day is the sabbath of the LORD thy God: in it thou shalt not do any work, thou, nor thy son, nor thy daughter, thy manservant, nor thy maidservant, nor thy cattle, nor thy stranger that is within thy gates:*

11   *For in six days the LORD made heaven and earth, the sea, and all that in them is, and rested the seventh day: wherefore the LORD blessed the sabbath day, and hallowed it.*

Overview

Our God is a creating God, and He has designed us to be creative and productive. Regular rest enhances energy and our capacity for accomplishment. It also renews our spirits by giving us the opportunity to focus on worshipping God.

Lesson Theme

Truly, one of the greatest challenges facing us today is the challenge to find rest. God, in His wisdom, provided for this basic need when He gave the fourth commandment as a pattern for balancing work and rest.

Introduction

_____

_____

_____

I. There Is Rest in a _Pattern_

EXODUS 20:8–10

8   Remember the sabbath day, to keep it holy.

9   Six days shalt thou labour, and do all thy work:

10   But the seventh day is the sabbath of the LORD thy God: in it thou shalt not do any work, thou, nor thy son, nor thy daughter, thy manservant, nor thy maidservant, nor thy cattle, nor thy stranger that is within thy gates:

A. The _pattern_ of work

PSALMS 33:6

6   By the word of the LORD were the heavens made; and all the host of them by the breath of his mouth.

EPHESIANS 2:10

10   For we are his workmanship, created in Christ Jesus unto good works, which God hath before ordained that we should walk in them.

B. The _partition_ of work

EXODUS 20:8, 11

8   Remember the sabbath day, to keep it holy.

11   For in six days the LORD made heaven and earth, the sea, and all that in them is, and rested the seventh day: wherefore the LORD blessed the sabbath day, and hallowed it.

1 CORINTHIANS 10:31

31   Whether therefore ye eat, or drink, or whatsoever ye do, do all to the glory of God.

II. There Is Rest in a <u>Practice</u>

EXODUS 20:9–10

9   Six days shalt thou labour, and do all thy work:
10   But the seventh day is the sabbath of the LORD thy God…

A. The <u>enjoyment</u> of completed work

GENESIS 2:2–3

2   And on the seventh day God ended his work which he had made; and he rested on the seventh day from all his work which he had made.
3   And God blessed the seventh day, and sanctified it: because that in it he had rested from all his work which God created and made.

MARK 6:31

31   And he said unto them, Come ye yourselves apart into a desert place, and rest a while: for there were many coming and going, and they had no leisure so much as to eat.

B. The _____ of completed work

ROMANS 12:2

2   And be not conformed to this world: but be ye transformed by the renewing of your mind, that ye may prove what is that good, and acceptable, and perfect, will of God.

HEBREWS 10:25

25 Not forsaking the assembling of ourselves together, as the manner of some is; but exhorting one another: and so much the more, as ye see the day approaching.

1. **Physical breakdown**

2. **Mental breakdown**

3. **Spiritual bankruptcy**

4. **Family difficulties**

III. There Is Rest in a Person

A. *His* forgiveness *offers rest.*

EPHESIANS 1:7

7 In whom we have redemption through his blood, the forgiveness of sins, according to the riches of his grace;

JOHN 10:28

28 And I give unto them eternal life; and they shall never perish, neither shall any man pluck them out of my hand.

B. *Our* faith *in Him brings salvation.*

EPHESIANS 2:8–9

8 For by grace are ye saved through faith; and that not of yourselves: it is the gift of God:

9 Not of works, lest any man should boast.

HEBREWS 4:2
2   For unto us was the gospel preached, as well as unto them: but the word preached did not profit them, not being mixed with faith in them that heard it.

Conclusion

JOHN 10:10
10 The thief cometh not, but for to steal, and to kill, and to destroy: I am come that they might have life, and that they might have it more abundantly.

_____

_____

_____

Study Questions

1. What need in our lives does the fourth commandment address?

2. How is God's attribute of order reflected in the fourth commandment?

3. How does rest enhance our productivity?

4. Why must church attendance be part of our sabbath rest?

5. When you understand that the work God has provided for you reflects His nature, your work will become more meaningful. What in your work reflects the nature of God?

6. What does your church attendance reflect about your priorities?

7.   What plan do you follow for daily renewal in God's Word?

8.   What do you need to remove from your life to make sabbath rest a priority?

Memory Verse

Hebrews 10:25

25 Not forsaking the assembling of ourselves together, as the manner of some is; but exhorting one another: and so much the more, as ye see the day approaching.

Keeping Family Honor

Text

EXODUS 20:12

12 Honour thy father and thy mother: that thy days may be long upon the land which the LORD thy God giveth thee.

Overview

The Ten Commandments have been a great priority for successful families and nations throughout the centuries. The fifth commandment is the only commandment to which God attaches a promise, and it is a key to the strength of a family and a nation.

Lesson Theme

God's design is for parents to guide their children through some of the difficult challenges of life. Obedience to the fifth commandment gives access to the blessings God intends to bestow through the parent/child relationship.

Introduction

_____

_____

_____

I. The Principle of _____ Honor

A. The principle of _first_ relation

B. The principle of _displaying_ honor

EPHESIANS 6:1
1 Children, obey your parents in the Lord: for this is right.

LUKE 2:51
51 And he went down with them, and came to Nazareth, and was subject unto them: but his mother kept all these sayings in her heart.

PROVERBS 30:17
17 The eye that mocketh at his father, and despiseth to obey his mother, the ravens of the valley shall pick it out, and the young eagles shall eat it.

PHILIPPIANS 2:14
14 Do all things without murmurings and disputings:

JOHN 19:26–27
26 When Jesus therefore saw his mother, and the disciple standing by, whom he loved, he saith unto his mother, Woman, behold thy son!

27 Then saith he to the disciple, Behold thy mother! And from that hour that disciple took her unto his own home.

II. The Problems of <u>Showing</u> Honor

A. When parents' <u>actions</u> are wrong

1 SAMUEL 20:33
33 And Saul cast a javelin at him to smite him: whereby Jonathan knew that it was determined of his father to slay David.

EPHESIANS 4:32
32 And be ye kind one to another, tenderhearted, forgiving one another, even as God for Christ's sake hath forgiven you.

2 CORINTHIANS 10:5
5 Casting down imaginations, and every high thing that exalteth itself against the knowledge of God, and bringing into captivity every thought to the obedience of Christ;

B. When parents' <u>advice</u> is wrong

PROVERBS 24:6
6 For by wise counsel thou shalt make thy war: and in multitude of counsellors there is safety.

III. The Priority of <u>Teaching</u> Honor

A. Remember your responsibility to <u>train</u>.

Ephesians 6:2–4

2   *Honour thy father and mother; (which is the first commandment with promise;)*

3   *That it may be well with thee, and thou mayest live long on the earth.*

4   *And, ye fathers, provoke not your children to wrath: but bring them up in the nurture and admonition of the Lord.*

Proverbs 29:15

15   *The rod and reproof give wisdom: but a child left to himself bringeth his mother to shame.*

Ephesians 4:15

15   *But speaking the truth in love, may grow up into him in all things, which is the head, even Christ:*

B. *Remember your responsibility to __pray__.*

James 1:5

5   *If any of you lack wisdom, let him ask of God, that giveth to all men liberally, and upbraideth not; and it shall be given him.*

Conclusion

Exodus 20:12

12   *Honour thy father and thy mother: that thy days may be long upon the land which the Lord thy God giveth thee.*

_____

_____

_____

Study Questions

1.   What does the word *honor* mean?

2.   How should young children, adolescents, and adults best show honor to their parents?

3.   What are the two keys to healing from the wounds inflicted by parents' actions?

4.   What Bible character, discussed in this lesson, had an unreasonable and angry father? Did his father's failures prevent him from living for God?

5.   What can you do this week to show your parents you remember and love them?

6.   Through this lesson, did you identify any specific problems in your relationship with your parents? If so, what can you do to overcome these challenges to obeying the fifth command?

7. Are there either prevailing attitudes or specific obstacles in your family life that could make obeying the fifth command a challenge to your children? How can you restore a proper relationship with your children?

8. How many times did you pray for your children last week? Do you know your children's specific needs? How can you better pray for your children?

Memory Verse

EPHESIANS 6:1–4

1   *Children, obey your parents in the Lord: for this is right.*
2   *Honour thy father and mother; (which is the first commandment with promise;)*
3   *That it may be well with thee, and thou mayest live long on the earth.*
4   *And, ye fathers, provoke not your children to wrath: but bring them up in the nurture and admonition of the Lord.*

Keeping Life Sacred

Text

EXODUS 20:13
13 Thou shalt not kill.

Overview

In giving the command, "Thou shalt not kill," God not only prohibits taking life, but also places much importance on life.

Lesson Theme

The sixth commandment prohibits physically taking another person's life. Jesus built on this command by forbidding the attitudes of anger and hatred that wound the spirit and kill relationships.

Introduction

_____

_____

_____

I. An Announcement to accept

A. We are (made) created in His image.

GENESIS 1:26–27

26 And God said, Let us make man in our image, after our likeness: and let them have dominion over the fish of the sea, and over the fowl of the air, and over the cattle, and over all the earth, and over every creeping thing that creepeth upon the earth.

27 So God created man in his own image, in the image of God created he him; male and female created he them.

B. Being in the image of God makes human life distinct.

GENESIS 9:1–3

1 And God blessed Noah and his sons, and said unto them, Be fruitful, and multiply, and replenish the earth.

2 And the fear of you and the dread of you shall be upon every beast of the earth, and upon every fowl of the air, upon all that moveth upon the earth, and upon all the fishes of the sea; into your hand are they delivered.

3 Every moving thing that liveth shall be meat for you; even as the green herb have I given you all things.

Matthew 6:26

26 Behold the fowls of the air: for they sow not, neither do they reap, nor gather into barns; yet your heavenly Father feedeth them. Are ye not much better than they?

Genesis 9:3

3 Every moving thing that liveth shall be meat for you; even as the green herb have I given you all things.

Genesis 9:6

6 Whoso sheddeth man's blood, by man shall his blood be shed: for in the image of God made he man.

1 Timothy 2:1–2

1 I exhort therefore, that, first of all, supplications, prayers, intercessions, and giving of thanks, be made for all men;
2 For kings, and for all that are in authority; that we may lead a quiet and peaceable life in all godliness and honesty.

II. An Application to _____

A. _____

Romans 12:19

19 Dearly beloved, avenge not yourselves, but rather give place unto wrath: for it is written, Vengeance is mine; I will repay, saith the Lord.

JOHN 18:10–11

10   Then Simon Peter having a sword drew it, and smote the high priest's servant, and cut off his right ear. The servant's name was Malchus.

11   Then said Jesus unto Peter, Put up thy sword into the sheath: the cup which my Father hath given me, shall I not drink it?

B.   Abortion

GENESIS 1:27

27   So God created man in his own image, in the image of God created he him; male and female created he them.

PSALMS 139:13–16

13   For thou hast possessed my reins: thou hast covered me in my mother's womb.

14   I will praise thee; for I am fearfully and wonderfully made: marvellous are thy works; and that my soul knoweth right well.

15   My substance was not hid from thee, when I was made in secret, and curiously wrought in the lowest parts of the earth.

16   Thine eyes did see my substance, yet being unperfect; and in thy book all my members were written, which in continuance were fashioned, when as yet there was none of them.

JEREMIAH 1:5

5   Before I formed thee in the belly I knew thee; and before thou camest forth out of the womb I sanctified thee, and I ordained thee a prophet unto the nations.

C.   Euthenasia

III. Attitudes to _Avoid_

A. An _____ attitude

MATTHEW 5:21–22
21 Ye have heard that it was said by them of old time, Thou shalt not kill; and whosoever shall kill shall be in danger of the judgment:
22 But I say unto you, That whosoever is angry with his brother without a cause shall be in danger of the judgment: and whosoever shall say to his brother, Raca, shall be in danger of the council: but whosoever shall say, Thou fool, shall be in danger of hell fire.

JAMES 1:20
20 For the wrath of man worketh not the righteousness of God.

1 PETER 5:7
7 Casting all your care upon him; for he careth for you.

EPHESIANS 4:31–32
31 Let all bitterness, and wrath, and anger, and clamour, and evil speaking, be put away from you, with all malice:
32 And be ye kind one to another, tenderhearted, forgiving one another, even as God for Christ's sake hath forgiven you.

EPHESIANS 4:26–27
26 Be ye angry, and sin not: let not the sun go down upon your wrath:
27 Neither give place to the devil.

B. A _hatefull_ *attitude*

1 JOHN 3:15
15 Whosoever hateth his brother is a murderer: and ye know that no murderer hath eternal life abiding in him.

1. **Humble yourself.**

2. **Have pure motives.**

3. **Seek forgiveness.**

4. **Pray together.**

   ROMANS 12:18
   18 If it be possible, as much as lieth in you, live peaceably with all men.

Conclusion

_____

_____

_____

Study Questions

1. What is the primary reason God places a distinction on human life?

2. What is the biblical penalty for murder?

3. What does Jeremiah 1:5 teach us about the unborn child?

4. Explain how euthanasia involves people playing the part of God?

5. Is there a person for whom you are harboring unresolved anger? How and when will you make the offense right?

6. In what situations are you most likely to display anger? What can you do before a situation arises to avoid it or to prepare yourself to respond in love?

7. What relationships in your life need to be mended? How are you going to implement the four ways to repair a broken relationship?

8. What can you do to build and strengthen a relationship this week?

Memory Verse

GENESIS 1:27
27 So God created man in his own image, in the image of God created he him; male and female created he them.

Keeping Purity

Text

EXODUS 20:14
14 Thou shalt not commit adultery.

Overview

The seventh commandment is about keeping a promise of sexual purity. This command obviously relates to the body, but the battle begins in the mind and in the heart.

Lesson Theme

God designed marriage to provide companionship and intimacy for a husband and a wife. Satan, however, has other plans. Just as he attempts to subvert every pure and beautiful creation of God, Satan seeks to destroy marriage. In this lesson we learn God's eight-step plan to make our marriages adultery-proof.

Introduction

_____

_____

_____

MATTHEW 5:27–28
27 Ye have heard that it was said by them of old time, Thou shalt not commit adultery:
28 But I say unto you, That whosoever looketh on a woman to lust after her hath committed adultery with her already in his heart.

I. God's ___plan___ for Marriage

GENESIS 1:27
27 So God created man in his own image, in the image of God created he him; male and female created he them.

A. *He designed marriage for* Companionship.

GENESIS 2:18
18 And the LORD God said, It is not good that the man should be alone; I will make him an help meet for him.

1 THESSALONIANS 5:23
23 And the very God of peace sanctify you wholly; and I pray God your whole spirit and soul and body be preserved blameless unto the coming of our Lord Jesus Christ.

PROVERBS 6:32

32 But whoso committeth adultery with a woman lacketh understanding: he that doeth it destroyeth his own soul.

B. He designed marriage for ___intimacy___.

GENESIS 2:24

24 Therefore shall a man leave his father and his mother, and shall cleave unto his wife: and they shall be one flesh.

HEBREWS 13:4

4 Marriage is honourable in all, and the bed undefiled: but whoremongers and adulterers God will judge.

II. Satan's ___plan___ against Marriage

1 PETER 5:8

5 Be sober, be vigilant; because your adversary the devil, as a roaring lion, walketh about, seeking whom he may devour:

A. Satan _____ to destroy.

JOHN 8:44

Ye are of your father the devil, and the lusts of your father ye will do. He was a murderer from the beginning, and abode not in the truth, because there is no truth in him. When he speaketh a lie, he speaketh of his own: for he is a liar, and the father of it.

1 THESSALONIANS 4:3–7

3   For this is the will of God, even your sanctification, that ye should abstain from fornication:

4   That every one of you should know how to possess his vessel in sanctification and honour;

5   Not in the lust of concupiscence, even as the Gentiles which know not God:

6   That no man go beyond and defraud his brother in any matter: because that the Lord is the avenger of all such, as we also have forewarned you and testified.

7   For God hath not called us unto uncleanness, but unto holiness.

B. Satan ___tempts___ **to destroy.**

JAMES 1:14–15

14   But every man is tempted, when he is drawn away of his own lust, and enticed.

15   Then when lust hath conceived, it bringeth forth sin: and sin, when it is finished, bringeth forth death.

III. God's Plan for an ___honourable___ Marriage

A. His ___priority___ **is purity.**

GENESIS 1:27

27   So God created man in his own image, in the image of God created he him; male and female created he them.

1 CORINTHIANS 6:20

20   For ye are bought with a price: therefore glorify God in your body, and in your spirit, which are God's.

1 CORINTHIANS 6:19

19   What? know ye not that your body is the temple of the Holy Ghost which is in you, which ye have of God, and ye are not your own?

ROMANS 12:1

1   I beseech you therefore, brethren, by the mercies of God, that ye present your bodies a living sacrifice, holy, acceptable unto God, which is your reasonable service.

B. He has a _____plan_____ for purity.

1.   Recognize _sin is_ against God.

GENESIS 39:7–9

7   And it came to pass after these things, that his master's wife cast her eyes upon Joseph; and she said, Lie with me.

8   But he refused, and said unto his master's wife, Behold, my master wotteth not what is with me in the house, and he hath committed all that he hath to my hand;

*9   There is none greater in this house than I; neither hath he kept back any thing from me but thee, because thou art his wife: how then can I do this great wickedness, and **sin against God**?*

PSALMS 51:4

4   Against thee, thee only, have I sinned, and done this evil in thy sight: that thou mightest be justified when thou speakest, and be clear when thou judgest.

2.   Rely on the Holy Spirit for _power_.

TITUS 2:11–12

11 For the grace of God that bringeth salvation hath appeared to all men,

12 Teaching us that, denying ungodliness and worldly lusts, we should live soberly, righteously, and godly, in this present world;

ROMANS 8:13

13 For if ye live after the flesh, ye shall die: but if ye through the Spirit do mortify the deeds of the body, ye shall live.

3. Fight the <u>fight</u>**!**

1 THESSALONIANS 4:7

7 For God hath not called us unto uncleanness, but unto holiness.

4. Minimize the <u>temptations</u>**.**

2 TIMOTHY 2:22

22 Flee also youthful lusts: but follow righteousness, faith, charity, peace, with them that call on the Lord out of a pure heart.

5. Maintain godly <u>friendships</u>**.**

1 CORINTHIANS 15:33

33 Be not deceived: evil communications corrupt good manners.

6. Don't <u>rationalize</u>**.**

PROVERBS 21:2

2   *Every way of a man is right in his own eyes: but the LORD pondereth the hearts.*

7. **Build your** _marriage_ .

EPHESIANS 5:33

33 *Nevertheless let every one of you in particular so love his wife even as himself; and the wife see that she reverence her husband.*

8. _Forgive_ .

Conclusion

JOHN 8:3–11

3   *And the scribes and Pharisees brought unto him a woman taken in adultery; and when they had set her in the midst,*

4   *They say unto him, Master, this woman was taken in adultery, in the very act.*

5   *Now Moses in the law commanded us, that such should be stoned: but what sayest thou?*

6   *This they said, tempting him, that they might have to accuse him. But Jesus stooped down, and with his finger wrote on the ground, as though he heard them not.*

7   *So when they continued asking him, he lifted up himself, and said unto them, He that is without sin among you, let him first cast a stone at her.*

8   *And again he stooped down, and wrote on the ground.*

9   *And they which heard it, being convicted by their own conscience, went out one by one, beginning at the eldest,*

even unto the last: and Jesus was left alone, and the woman standing in the midst.

10 When Jesus had lifted up himself, and saw none but the woman, he said unto her, Woman, where are those thine accusers? hath no man condemned thee?

11 She said, No man, Lord. And Jesus said unto her, Neither do I condemn thee: go, and sin no more.

_____

_____

_____

Study Questions

1. What are God's two primary purposes for marriage?

2. What three aspects of our beings should comprise marital companionship, and what needs does each represent?

3. What does Satan use to destroy marriages?

4. List the eight steps given to affair-proof your marriage.

5. How can you best meet the companionship needs of your spouse?

6. Did you identify specific lies or temptations Satan is using to destroy your marriage?

7. What steps can you take to minimize the temptation of impurity?

8. What can you do this week to build your marriage?

Memory Verse

1 THESSALONIANS 5:23
23 And the very God of peace sanctify you wholly; and I pray God your whole spirit and soul and body be preserved blameless unto the coming of our Lord Jesus Christ.

Keeping Integrity

Text

Exodus 20:15

15 Thou shalt not steal.

Overview

The eighth commandment addresses much more than taking an object that does not belong to you. It addresses the need for integrity—where we work, where we live, and where we worship.

Lesson Theme

Developing a high standard of personal integrity poses a great challenge, but the Christian who accepts the challenge and overcomes it through the power of the Holy Spirit will circumvent the greater challenges created by a lack of integrity.

Introduction

_____

_____

_____

I. Keeping Integrity Where You <u>Work</u>

A. When employees <u>give</u> their best

EPHESIANS 4:28

*28 Let him that stole steal no more: but rather let him
labour, working with his hands the thing which is good,
that he may have to give to him that needeth.*

COLOSSIANS 3:22–23

*22 Servants, obey in all things your masters according
to the flesh; not with eyeservice, as menpleasers; but in
singleness of heart, fearing God:*
*23 And whatsoever ye do, do it heartily, as to the Lord,
and not unto men;*

B. When employers <u>bless</u> their employees

COLOSSIANS 4:1

*Masters, give unto your servants that which is just and
equal; knowing that ye also have a Master in heaven.*

PROVERBS 3:27

*27 Withhold not good from them to whom it is due,
when it is in the power of thine hand to do it.*

JAMES 5:4

*4 Behold, the hire of the labourers who have reaped
down your fields, which is of you kept back by fraud,*

crieth: and the cries of them which have reaped are entered into the ears of the Lord of sabaoth.

II. Keeping Integrity Where You <u>Live</u>

A. Pay your <u>loans</u>.

1. Don't <u>charge</u>, hoping the money will be there at the end of the month.

2. Practice <u>contentment</u>.

PROVERBS 15:16–17
16 Better is little with the fear of the LORD than great treasure and trouble therewith.
17 Better is a dinner of herbs where love is, than a stalled ox and hatred therewith.

3. <u>Pray</u> before you buy.

PROVERBS 21:5
5 The thoughts of the diligent tend only to plenteousness; but of every one that is hasty only to want.

B. Make <u>restitution</u>.

LUKE 19:8
8 And Zacchaeus stood, and said unto the Lord; Behold, Lord, the half of my goods I give to the poor; and if I have taken any thing from any man by false accusation, I restore him fourfold.

C. *Make a* _fair_ *and* _honest_ *living.*

AMOS 8:5

5   *Saying, When will the new moon be gone, that we may sell corn? and the sabbath, that we may set forth wheat, making the ephah small, and the shekel great, and falsifying the balances by deceit?*

PROVERBS 13:11

11   *Wealth gotten by vanity shall be diminished: but he that gathereth by labour shall increase.*

III. Keeping Integrity Where We _Worship_

JEREMIAH 7:9–11

9   *Will ye steal, murder, and commit adultery, and swear falsely, and burn incense unto Baal, and walk after other gods whom ye know not;*

10   **And come and stand before me in this house,** *which is called by my name, and say, We are delivered to do all these abominations?*

11   *Is this house, which is called by my name, become a den of robbers in your eyes? Behold, even I have seen it, saith the LORD.*

ISAIAH 42:8

8   *I am the LORD: that is my name: and my glory will I not give to another, neither my praise to graven images.*

A. *Integrity in our* _message_

JOHN 17:17

17 *Sanctify them through thy truth: thy word is truth.*

2 Timothy 4:2–3

2   Preach the word; be instant in season, out of season; reprove, rebuke, exhort with all longsuffering and doctrine.

3   For the time will come when they will not endure sound doctrine; but after their own lusts shall they heap to themselves teachers, having itching ears;

1 Thessalonians 2:3–5

3   For our exhortation was not of deceit, nor of uncleanness, nor in guile:

4   But as we were allowed of God to be put in trust with the gospel, even so we speak; not as pleasing men, but God, which trieth our hearts.

5   For neither at any time used we flattering words, as ye know, nor a cloke of covetousness; God is witness:

B.   ***Integrity in our*** testimony

Philippians 1:27

27   Only let your conversation be as it becometh the gospel of Christ: that whether I come and see you, or else be absent, I may hear of your affairs, that ye stand fast in one spirit, with one mind striving together for the faith of the gospel;

2 Corinthians 4:1–2

1   Therefore seeing we have this ministry, as we have received mercy, we faint not;

2   But have renounced the hidden things of dishonesty, not walking in craftiness, nor handling the word of God deceitfully; but by manifestation of the truth commending ourselves to every man's conscience in the sight of God.

C. *Integrity in our* giving

MALACHI 3:8–10

8   Will a man rob God? Yet ye have robbed me. But ye say, Wherein have we robbed thee? In tithes and offerings.

9   Ye are cursed with a curse: for ye have robbed me, even this whole nation.

10   Bring ye all the tithes into the storehouse, that there may be meat in mine house, and prove me now herewith, saith the LORD of hosts, if I will not open you the windows of heaven, and pour you out a blessing, that there shall not be room enough to receive it.

1 CORINTHIANS 4:2

2   Moreover it is required in stewards, that a man be found faithful.

Conclusion

_____

_____

_____

Study Questions

1. List four ways employees commonly steal from their employers?

2. What are the three steps to avoiding debt?

3. What is the standard of truth we must use to maintain integrity in our message?

4. How is tithing an act of worship?

5. In what ways is your testimony to your employer, coworkers, employees, or customers a reflection of your integrity or lack thereof?

6. To whom do you owe money? What is your plan to pay your current outstanding loans?

7. One statement in our lesson reads, "Integrity is keeping my commitment even when the circumstances surrounding my commitment have changed." What commitments have you neglected because of a change in circumstances?

8. To whom do you need to make restitution for a past lack of integrity? What steps will you take toward restitution this week?

Memory Verse
EPHESIANS 4:28
28 Let him that stole steal no more: but rather let him labour, working with his hands the thing which is good, that he may have to give to him that needeth.

Keeping Truth

Text

EXODUS 20:16

16 Thou shalt not bear false witness against thy neighbour.

Overview

Lying and deceit have become accepted and even expected in our society. This distortion of truth is no accident; it is the outcome of Satan's deliberate plot against the truth. Keeping the truth in a world bent on falsehood is a challenge, but it's a challenge worth giving your all. And keeping the truth is sure to bring victory, because the truth itself has power to free those who believe and receive it.

Lesson Theme

The ninth commandment calls us all back to the pathway of truth.

Introduction

_____

_____

_____

PROVERBS 6:16–19

16 *These six things doth the LORD hate: yea, seven are an abomination unto him:*

17 *A proud look, a lying tongue, and hands that shed innocent blood,*

18 *An heart that deviseth wicked imaginations, feet that be swift in running to mischief,*

19 *A false witness that speaketh lies, and he that soweth discord among brethren.*

TITUS 1:2

2 *In hope of eternal life, which God, that cannot lie, promised before the world began;*

I.   The _____ against the Truth

A. *Satan _____ the truth.*

GENESIS 3:1

1 *Now the serpent was more subtil than any beast of the field which the LORD God had made. And he said unto the woman, Yea, hath God said, Ye shall not eat of every tree of the garden?*

GENESIS 3:4

4 *And the serpent said unto the woman, Ye shall not surely die:*

JOHN 8:44

44 Ye are of your father the devil, and the lusts of your father ye will do. He was a murderer from the beginning, and abode not in the truth, because there is no truth in him. When he speaketh a lie, he speaketh of his own: for he is a liar, and the father of it.

B. Unbelieving culture _____ the truth.

ISAIAH 5:20

20 Woe unto them that call evil good, and good evil; that put darkness for light, and light for darkness; that put bitter for sweet, and sweet for bitter!

ROMANS 1:25–27

25 Who changed the truth of God into a lie, and worshipped and served the creature more than the Creator, who is blessed for ever. Amen.

26 For this cause God gave them up unto vile affections: for even their women did change the natural use into that which is against nature:

27 And likewise also the men, leaving the natural use of the woman, burned in their lust one toward another; men with men working that which is unseemly, and receiving in themselves that recompence of their error which was meet.

II. The _____ of Truth Rejecters

A. They resist _____ truth.

JOHN 18:37

37 Pilate therefore said unto him, Art thou a king then? Jesus answered, Thou sayest that I am a king.

To this end was I born, and for this cause came I into the world, that I should bear witness unto the truth. Every one that is of the truth heareth my voice.

John 18:38
38 Pilate saith unto him, What is truth? And when he had said this, he went out again unto the Jews, and saith unto them, I find in him no fault at all.

B. *They reject _____ truth.*

Proverbs 12:19–20
19 The lip of truth shall be established for ever: but a lying tongue is but for a moment.
20 Deceit is in the heart of them that imagine evil: but to the counsellors of peace is joy.

1. **To get revenge**

2. **To make a profit**

3. **To escape punishment**

4. **To impress people**

C. *They rearrange _____ truth.*

1. **False speech**

2. **Malicious accusation**

Proverbs 15:28
28 The heart of the righteous studieth to answer: but the mouth of the wicked poureth out evil things.

3. Slander

PROVERBS 12:17
17 He that speaketh truth sheweth forth righteousness: but a false witness deceit.

LUKE 7:34
34 The Son of man is come eating and drinking; and ye say, Behold a gluttonous man, and a winebibber, a friend of publicans and sinners!

PROVERBS 20:19
19 He that goeth about as a talebearer revealeth secrets: therefore meddle not with him that flattereth with his lips.

D. *They ruin lives by _____ the truth.*

JAMES 3:5–6
5 Even so the tongue is a little member, and boasteth great things. Behold, how great a matter a little fire kindleth!
6 And the tongue is a fire, a world of iniquity: so is the tongue among our members, that it defileth the whole body, and setteth on fire the course of nature; and it is set on fire of hell.

1. Pray for the one who gossiped.

2. Speak kindly to them.

EPHESIANS 4:15
15 But speaking the truth in love, may grow up into him in all things, which is the head, even Christ:

Proverbs 15:1

1   A soft answer turneth away wrath: but grievous words stir up anger.

3.   Be honest toward them.

James 5:12

12 But above all things, my brethren, swear not, neither by heaven, neither by the earth, neither by any other oath: but let your yea be yea; and your nay, nay; lest ye fall into condemnation.

4.   Forgive them.

Proverbs 26:20

20 Where no wood is, there the fire goeth out: so where there is no talebearer, the strife ceaseth.

III. The _____ to Truth

A.   *We know the truth through the _____.*

John 17:17

17 Sanctify them through thy truth: thy word is truth.

1 Peter 1:23–25

23 Being born again, not of corruptible seed, but of incorruptible, by the word of God, which liveth and abideth for ever.
24 For all flesh is as grass, and all the glory of man as the flower of grass. The grass withereth, and the flower thereof falleth away:

25 But the word of the Lord endureth for ever. And this is the word which by the gospel is preached unto you.

JOHN 14:6
6 Jesus saith unto him, I am the way, the truth, and the life: no man cometh unto the Father, but by me.

PSALM 119:138
138 Thy testimonies that thou hast commanded are righteous and very faithful.

HEBREWS 4:12
12 For the word of God is quick, and powerful, and sharper than any twoedged sword, piercing even to the dividing asunder of soul and spirit, and of the joints and marrow, and is a discerner of the thoughts and intents of the heart.

MATTHEW 24:34–35
34 Verily I say unto you, This generation shall not pass, till all these things be fulfilled.
35 Heaven and earth shall pass away, but my words shall not pass away.

B. *We know the truth through* _____.

JOHN 14:6
6 Jesus saith unto him, I am the way, the truth, and the life: no man cometh unto the Father, but by me.

JOHN 8:31–32
31 Then said Jesus to those Jews which believed on him, If ye continue in my word, then are ye my disciples indeed;

32   And ye shall know the truth, and the truth shall make you free.

ROMANS 5:8
8   But God commendeth his love toward us, in that, while we were yet sinners, Christ died for us.

JOHN 3:16–18
16   For God so loved the world, that he gave his only begotten Son, that whosoever believeth in him should not perish, but have everlasting life.
17   For God sent not his Son into the world to condemn the world; but that the world through him might be saved.
18   He that believeth on him is not condemned: but he that believeth not is condemned already, because he hath not believed in the name of the only begotten Son of God.

Conclusion

_____

_____

_____

Study Questions

1. According to this lesson, why does God hate lying so much?

2. What is Satan's most effective strategy against the truth?

3. List the three ways people bear false witness.

4. Why is searching for truth from any source other than God's Word foolish?

5. What are some ways you have seen culture change the truth in your lifetime?

6. Do you have a relationship that has been damaged by someone's slandering your name? If so, what steps will you take this week to restore that relationship?

7. Do people feel comfortable bearing false witness about others to you? What can you do to prevent slanderers from coming to you?

8. In what area of your life do you need God's truth? Does your Bible study reflect a hunger for this truth?

Memory Verse

JOHN 8:32
32 And ye shall know the truth, and the truth shall make you free.

Keeping Contentment

Text

EXODUS 20:4–5

4   Thou shalt not make unto thee any graven image, or any likeness of any thing that is in heaven above, or that is in the earth beneath, or that is in the water under the earth:

5   Thou shalt not bow down thyself to them, nor serve them: for I the LORD thy God am a jealous God, visiting the iniquity of the fathers upon the children unto the third and fourth generation of them that hate me;

Overview

The first of the Ten Commandments was the command to put God first in our lives, and the last is a warning not to allow any coveted thing to usurp God's rightful place. It is a command to be satisfied with God Himself and to enjoy the blessings He gives us as a bonus.

Lesson Theme

If we were to define contentment in our own terms, we would have a much narrower definition than what God's Word gives. Studying biblical contentment is convicting. It challenges us to inspect our hearts and lives for anything that is taking God's place, and it motivates us to put God first.

Introduction

_____

_____

_____

EXODUS 20:17
17 Thou shalt not covet thy neighbour's house, thou shalt not covet thy neighbour's wife, nor his manservant, nor his maidservant, nor his ox, nor his ass, nor any thing that is thy neighbour's.

1 PETER 3:3–4
3   Whose adorning let it not be that outward adorning of plaiting the hair, and of wearing of gold, or of putting on of apparel;
4   But let it be the hidden man of the heart, in that which is not corruptible, even the ornament of a meek and quiet spirit, which is in the sight of God of great price.

LUKE 12:15
15 And he said unto them, Take heed, and beware of covetousness: for a man's life consisteth not in the abundance of the things which he possesseth.

I.   The _____ of Contentment

A. *My heart is _____.*

PSALMS 57:7
7   My heart is fixed, O God, my heart is fixed: I will sing and give praise.

MATTHEW 5:8

8 Blessed are the pure in heart: for they shall see God.

COLOSSIANS 3:5–6

5 Mortify therefore your members which are upon the earth; fornication, uncleanness, inordinate affection, evil concupiscence, and covetousness, which is idolatry:
6 For which things' sake the wrath of God cometh on the children of disobedience:

B. My focus is _____.

COLOSSIANS 3:1–2

1 If ye then be risen with Christ, seek those things which are above, where Christ sitteth on the right hand of God.
2 Set your affection on things above, not on things on the earth.

1 CORINTHIANS 10:31

31 Whether therefore ye eat, or drink, or whatsoever ye do, do all to the glory of God.

C. My trust is in _____.

MATTHEW 6:33

33 But seek ye first the kingdom of God, and his righteousness; and all these things shall be added unto you.

D. My life is _____.

LUKE 18:18–24

18 And a certain ruler asked him, saying, Good Master, what shall I do to inherit eternal life?

19 And Jesus said unto him, Why callest thou me good? none is good, save one, that is, God.

20 Thou knowest the commandments, Do not commit adultery, Do not kill, Do not steal, Do not bear false witness, Honour thy father and thy mother.

21 And he said, All these have I kept from my youth up.

22 Now when Jesus heard these things, he said unto him, Yet lackest thou one thing: sell all that thou hast, and distribute unto the poor, and thou shalt have treasure in heaven: and come, follow me.

23 And when he heard this, he was very sorrowful: for he was very rich.

24 And when Jesus saw that he was very sorrowful, he said, How hardly shall they that have riches enter into the kingdom of God!

II. The _____ of Contentment

A. *Don't neglect your _____.*

PROVERBS 22:1

1 A good name is rather to be chosen than great riches, and loving favour rather than silver and gold.

EXODUS 20:17

17 ...thou shalt not covet thy neighbour's wife...

B. *Don't lose your _____.*

EPHESIANS 5:15

15 See then that ye walk circumspectly, not as fools, but as wise,

1. Fatigue

PROVERBS 23:4
4 Labour not to be rich: cease from thine own wisdom.

2. Dissatisfaction

ECCLESIASTES 5:10
10 He that loveth silver shall not be satisfied with silver; nor he that loveth abundance with increase: this is also vanity.

3. Debt

PROVERBS 17:1
1 Better is a dry morsel, and quietness therewith, than an house full of sacrifices with strife.

4. Worry

MARK 4:18–19
18 And these are they which are sown among thorns; such as hear the word,
19 And the cares of this world, and the deceitfulness of riches, and the lusts of other things entering in, choke the word, and it becometh unfruitful.

5. Conflict

JAMES 4:1–2
1 From whence come wars and fightings among you? come they not hence, even of your lusts that war in your members?

2   Ye lust, and have not: ye kill, and desire to have, and cannot obtain: ye fight and war, yet ye have not, because ye ask not.

C. Don't ruin _____.

JAMES 4:1
1   From whence come wars and fightings among you? come they not hence, even of your lusts that war in your members?

D. Don't lose your _____.

1 TIMOTHY 6:9–10
9   But they that will be rich fall into temptation and a snare, and into many foolish and hurtful lusts, which drown men in destruction and perdition.
10   For the love of money is the root of all evil: which while some coveted after, they have erred from the faith, and pierced themselves through with many sorrows.

III. The _____ of Contentment

PHILIPPIANS 4:11–12
11   Not that I speak in respect of want: for I have learned, in whatsoever state I am, therewith to be content.
12   I know both how to be abased, and I know how to abound: every where and in all things I am instructed both to be full and to be hungry, both to abound and to suffer need.

A. Thankful for God's blessing to _____

EXODUS 20:17

17 Thou shalt not covet thy neighbour's house, thou shalt not covet thy neighbour's wife, nor his manservant, nor his maidservant, nor his ox, nor his ass, nor any thing that is thy neighbour's.

HEBREWS 13:5–6

5 Let your conversation be without covetousness; and be content with such things as ye have: for he hath said, I will never leave thee, nor forsake thee.
6 So that we may boldly say, The Lord is my helper, and I will not fear what man shall do unto me.

JOB 1:21

21 And said, Naked came I out of my mother's womb, and naked shall I return thither: the LORD gave, and the LORD hath taken away; blessed be the name of the LORD.

B. *Thankful for God's blessing on* _____

ROMANS 12:15

15 Rejoice with them that do rejoice, and weep with them that weep.

C. *Thankful in our* _____

2 CORINTHIANS 9:7

7 Every man according as he purposeth in his heart, so let him give; not grudgingly, or of necessity: for God loveth a cheerful giver.

PROVERBS 28:27

27 He that giveth unto the poor shall not lack: but he that hideth his eyes shall have many a curse.

D. *Thankful in our* _____

Conclusion

_____

_____

_____

Study Questions

1. Why is covetousness the same as idolatry?

2. When our focus is heavenward, we will primarily structure our lives around that which lasts for eternity. What are two such things?

3. Explain this statement: Constant dissatisfaction is not an indicator of having too little; it is an indicator of looking for fulfillment in the wrong places.

4. Scripture highlights the lives of godly men who were wealthy. Do their lives violate the warning given in 1 Timothy 6:9–10? Why or why not?

5. In what ways have you structured your life around eternal values? Or in what ways do you need to restructure your life around eternal values?

6. Which of the convictions that maintain contentment do you need to give special attention to this week?

7. Which of the five indicators of a need for balance do you see in your life?

8. In what way does your giving reflect generosity or covetousness?

Memory Verse

PHILIPPIANS 4:11

11 Not that I speak in respect of want: for I have learned, in whatsoever state I am, therewith to be content.

Keeping the Great Commandment

Text

MATTHEW 22:34–40

34 But when the Pharisees had heard that he had put the Sadducees to silence, they were gathered together.

35 Then one of them, which was a lawyer, asked him a question, tempting him, and saying,

36 Master, which is the great commandment in the law?

37 Jesus said unto him, Thou shalt love the Lord thy God with all thy heart, and with all thy soul, and with all thy mind.

38 This is the first and great commandment.

39 And the second is like unto it, Thou shalt love thy neighbour as thyself.

40 On these two commandments hang all the law and the prophets.

Overview

The great commandment is a commandment to love. God does not want us merely to make a list of "thou shalts" and "thou shalt nots." His desire for us is that we would enter into a real and vibrant heart relationship with Him.

Lesson Theme

Because love is the strongest motivator in the universe, keeping God's commandments must be an expression of our love for God. God Himself has initiated a love relationship with us, and He desires for us to love Him with our entire being. This is the Great Commandment, and it is the key to overcoming life's greatest challenges.

Introduction

_____

_____

_____

MATTHEW 22:37–38
37 Jesus said unto him, Thou shalt love the Lord thy God with all thy heart, and with all thy soul, and with all thy mind.
38 This is the first and great commandment.

DEUTERONOMY 6:4–5
4 Hear, O Israel: The LORD our God is one LORD:
5 And thou shalt love the LORD thy God with all thine heart, and with all thy soul, and with all thy might.

I. A _____ Love

A. By _____ His love

1 JOHN 4:18–19
18 There is no fear in love; but perfect love casteth out fear: because fear hath torment. He that feareth is not made perfect in love.
19 We love him, because he first loved us.

B. By _____ His gift

1 JOHN 3:23
23 And this is his commandment, That we should believe on the name of his Son Jesus Christ, and love one another, as he gave us commandment.

1 JOHN 4:8–9

8 He that loveth not knoweth not God; for God is love.

9 In this was manifested the love of God toward us, because that God sent his only begotten Son into the world, that we might live through him.

JOHN 14:6

6 Jesus saith unto him, I am the way, the truth, and the life: no man cometh unto the Father, but by me.

C. By _____ His Word

LUKE 24:44

44 And he said unto them, These are the words which I spake unto you, while I was yet with you, that all things must be fulfilled, which were written in the law of Moses, and in the prophets, and in the psalms, concerning me.

JOHN 5:39

39 Search the scriptures; for in them ye think ye have eternal life: and they are they which testify of me.

II. A _____ Love

A. Our whole _____

MATTHEW 15:18–20

18 But those things which proceed out of the mouth come forth from the heart; and they defile the man.

19 For out of the heart proceed evil thoughts, murders, adulteries, fornications, thefts, false witness, blasphemies:

20 These are the things which defile a man: but to eat with unwashen hands defileth not a man.

JEREMIAH 29:13
13 And ye shall seek me, and find me, when ye shall search for me with all your heart.

1. Through our singing

EPHESIANS 5:18
18 And be not drunk with wine, wherein is excess; but be filled with the Spirit;
19 Speaking to yourselves in psalms and hymns and spiritual songs, singing and making melody in your heart to the Lord;

2. Through our giving

MATTHEW 6:21
21 For where your treasure is, there will your heart be also.

3. Through our Bible reading

PSALMS 119:111–112
111 Thy testimonies have I taken as an heritage for ever: for they are the rejoicing of my heart.
112 I have inclined mine heart to perform thy statutes alway, even unto the end.

4. Through our serving

2 CORINTHIANS 5:14
14 For the love of Christ constraineth us; because we thus judge, that if one died for all, then were all dead:

B. Our whole _____

PSALMS 139:14

14   I will praise thee; for I am fearfully and wonderfully made: marvellous are thy works; and that my soul knoweth right well.

PSALMS 34:2

2   My soul shall make her boast in the LORD: the humble shall hear thereof, and be glad.

C. Our whole _____

2 CORINTHIANS 10:5

5   Casting down imaginations, and every high thing that exalteth itself against the knowledge of God, and bringing into captivity every thought to the obedience of Christ;

ROMANS 12:2

2   And be not conformed to this world: but be ye transformed by the renewing of your mind, that ye may prove what is that good, and acceptable, and perfect, will of God.

III. An _____ Love

MATTHEW 22:39

39   And the second is like unto it, Thou shalt love thy neighbour as thyself.

ROMANS 13:8–9

8   Owe no man any thing, but to love one another: for he that loveth another hath fulfilled the law.

9   For this, Thou shalt not commit adultery, Thou shalt not kill, Thou shalt not steal, Thou shalt not bear false witness, Thou shalt not covet; and if there be any other commandment, it is briefly comprehended in this saying, namely, Thou shalt love thy neighbour as thyself.

A. A _____ love

1 CORINTHIANS 13:4
*4   Charity suffereth long, **and is kind**; charity envieth not; charity vaunteth not itself, is not puffed up,*

1 JOHN 4:20–21
20   If a man say, I love God, and hateth his brother, he is a liar: for he that loveth not his brother whom he hath seen, how can he love God whom he hath not seen?
21   And this commandment have we from him, That he who loveth God love his brother also.

B. A _____ love

1 CORINTHIANS 13:5
*5   Doth not behave itself unseemly, **seeketh not her own**, is not easily provoked, thinketh no evil;*

JOHN 13:34–35
34   A new commandment I give unto you, That ye love one another; as I have loved you, that ye also love one another.
35   By this shall all men know that ye are my disciples, if ye have love one to another.

C. An _____ love

1 CORINTHIANS 13:7
7   Beareth all things, believeth all things, hopeth all things, endureth all things.

Conclusion

_____

_____

_____

Study Questions

1. What is God's "love letter" to you?

2. List the four ways that we focus our hearts on God?

3. What is necessary if we are to consistently love God with our whole minds?

4. The world's love is expressed in this philosophy: "You scratch my back, and I'll scratch your back." How is godly love expressed?

5. When did you begin a personal relationship with God through Christ? Describe as many specifics as you remember. (If you are not positive you have trusted Christ as your Saviour, or if you have questions, ask your class teacher.)

6. How often this week have you spent time renewing your mind and growing in your love for God by reading His love letter to you?

7. On a scale of one to ten, how devoted are you in your love for God? (Remember your love is most clearly expressed in your actions.) How can you grow in your love?

8. How will you display an active love for God this week? Who can you serve, and what will be your plan to serve them?

Memory Verse

JEREMIAH 29:13
13 And ye shall seek me, and find me, when ye shall search for me with all your heart.

LESSON TWELVE
Keeping Victory

Text

ROMANS 8:35–39

35 Who shall separate us from the love of Christ? shall tribulation, or distress, or persecution, or famine, or nakedness, or peril, or sword?

36 As it is written, For thy sake we are killed all the day long; we are accounted as sheep for the slaughter.

37 Nay, in all these things we are more than conquerors through him that loved us.

38 For I am persuaded, that neither death, nor life, nor angels, nor principalities, nor powers, nor things present, nor things to come,

39 Nor height, nor depth, nor any other creature, shall be able to separate us from the love of God, which is in Christ Jesus our Lord.

Overview

Life comes with a myriad of challenges. When we attempt to overcome these challenges in our own strength and with our own wisdom, we become overwhelmed, confused, disillusioned, and defeated.

But God gives us the resources and abilities to overcome these challenges through His truth. In the past eleven lessons, we examined these challenge-hurdling truths as we studied God's commands. In this lesson we will briefly revisit each command to refresh our memories and retune our focus.

Lesson Theme

When we approach life's greatest challenges with the mighty truths of God's Word and from the stance of our relationship in Christ, we not only *overcome* these challenges, we *more than* overcome. We become "more than conquerors."

Our greatest challenges are God's opportunities to display the greatness of His power through us. It is these challenges that give us the opportunity to render to our Lord obedience from our hearts. And it is these challenges that give us the opportunity to experience the strength and commitment of God's love, giving us victory.

Introduction

_____

_____

_____

I. Keeping God _____

EXODUS 20:2–3

2   I am the LORD thy God, which have brought thee out of the land of Egypt, out of the house of bondage.

3   Thou shalt have no other gods before me.

II. Keeping Our Worship _____

EXODUS 20:4–5

4   Thou shalt not make unto thee any graven image, or any likeness of any thing that is in heaven above, or that is in the earth beneath, or that is in the water under the earth:

5   Thou shalt not bow down thyself to them, nor serve them: for I the LORD thy God am a jealous God, visiting the iniquity of the fathers upon the children unto the third and fourth generation of them that hate me;

PSALMS 115:5–7

5   They have mouths, but they speak not: eyes have they, but they see not:

6   They have ears, but they hear not: noses have they, but they smell not:

7   They have hands, but they handle not: feet have they, but they walk not: neither speak they through their throat.

III. Keeping His Name _____

EXODUS 20:7

7   Thou shalt not take the name of the LORD thy God
in vain; for the LORD will not hold him guiltless that
taketh his name in vain.

JOB 1:20–21

20   Then Job arose, and rent his mantle, and shaved his
head, and fell down upon the ground, and worshipped,
21   And said, Naked came I out of my mother's womb,
and naked shall I return thither: the LORD gave, and
the LORD hath taken away; blessed be the name of
the LORD.

IV. Keeping His _____ Rest

EXODUS 20:8–11

8   Remember the sabbath day, to keep it holy.
9   Six days shalt thou labour, and do all thy work:
10   But the seventh day is the sabbath of the LORD thy
God: in it thou shalt not do any work, thou, nor thy son,
nor thy daughter, thy manservant, nor thy maidservant,
nor thy cattle, nor thy stranger that is within thy gates:
11   For in six days the LORD made heaven and earth,
the sea, and all that in them is, and rested the seventh
day: wherefore the LORD blessed the sabbath day, and
hallowed it.

HEBREWS 10:25

25   Not forsaking the assembling of ourselves together,
as the manner of some is; but exhorting one another:
and so much the more, as ye see the day approaching.

V. Keeping Family _____

Exodus 20:12

12 Honour thy father and thy mother: that thy days may be long upon the land which the LORD thy God giveth thee.

VI. Keeping Life _____

Exodus 20:13

13 Thou shalt not kill.

Ephesians 4:31–32

31 Let all bitterness, and wrath, and anger, and clamour, and evil speaking, be put away from you, with all malice:
32 And be ye kind one to another, tenderhearted, forgiving one another, even as God for Christ's sake hath forgiven you.

VII. Keeping _____

Exodus 20:14

14 Thou shalt not commit adultery.

Matthew 5:27–28

27 Ye have heard that it was said by them of old time, Thou shalt not commit adultery:
28 But I say unto you, That whosoever looketh on a woman to lust after her hath committed adultery with her already in his heart.

VIII. Keeping _____

Exodus 20:15

15 Thou shalt not steal.

IX. Keeping _____

EXODUS 20:16

16 *Thou shalt not bear false witness against thy neighbour.*

PROVERBS 12:19–20

19 *The lip of truth shall be established for ever: but a lying tongue is but for a moment.*
20 *Deceit is in the heart of them that imagine evil: but to the counsellors of peace is joy.*

MATTHEW 24:35

35 *Heaven and earth shall pass away, but my words shall not pass away.*

HEBREWS 4:12

12 *For the word of God is quick, and powerful, and sharper than any twoedged sword, piercing even to the dividing asunder of soul and spirit, and of the joints and marrow, and is a discerner of the thoughts and intents of the heart.*

JAMES 1:22–25

22 *But be ye doers of the word, and not hearers only, deceiving your own selves.*
23 *For if any be a hearer of the word, and not a doer, he is like unto a man beholding his natural face in a glass:*
24 *For he beholdeth himself, and goeth his way, and straightway forgetteth what manner of man he was.*
25 *But whoso looketh into the perfect law of liberty, and continueth therein, he being not a forgetful hearer, but a doer of the work, this man shall be blessed in his deed.*

LESSON TWELVE—KEEPING VICTORY

X. Keeping _____

EXODUS 20:17

17 Thou shalt not covet thy neighbour's house, thou shalt not covet thy neighbour's wife, nor his manservant, nor his maidservant, nor his ox, nor his ass, nor any thing that is thy neighbour's.

COLOSSIANS 3:5–6

5 Mortify therefore your members which are upon the earth; fornication, uncleanness, inordinate affection, evil concupiscence, and covetousness, which is idolatry:
6 For which things' sake the wrath of God cometh on the children of disobedience:

XI. Keeping the Great _____

MATTHEW 22:34–40

34 But when the Pharisees had heard that he had put the Sadducees to silence, they were gathered together.
35 Then one of them, which was a lawyer, asked him a question, tempting him, and saying,
36 Master, which is the great commandment in the law?
37 Jesus said unto him, Thou shalt love the Lord thy God with all thy heart, and with all thy soul, and with all thy mind.
38 This is the first and great commandment.
39 And the second is like unto it, Thou shalt love thy neighbour as thyself.
40 On these two commandments hang all the law and the prophets.

Conclusion

EPHESIANS 3:20

20 Now unto him that is able to do exceeding abundantly above all that we ask or think, according to the power that worketh in us,

EPHESIANS 1:18–19

18 The eyes of your understanding being enlightened; that ye may know what is the hope of his calling, and what the riches of the glory of his inheritance in the saints,

19 And what is the exceeding greatness of his power to us-ward who believe, according to the working of his mighty power,

ROMANS 8:35–39

35 Who shall separate us from the love of Christ? shall tribulation, or distress, or persecution, or famine, or nakedness, or peril, or sword?

36 As it is written, For thy sake we are killed all the day long; we are accounted as sheep for the slaughter.

37 Nay, in all these things we are more than conquerors through him that loved us.

38 For I am persuaded, that neither death, nor life, nor angels, nor principalities, nor powers, nor things present, nor things to come,

39 Nor height, nor depth, nor any other creature, shall be able to separate us from the love of God, which is in Christ Jesus our Lord.

_____

_____

_____

Study Questions

1. What is the result when we attempt to overcome life's challenges in our own strength and with our own wisdom?

2. What resources has God given us to overcome life's challenges?

3. The Christian life is not about _____; it is about a _____ with God Himself. It is not about the _____; it is about the _____.

4. What gives God the opportunity to display His power through us, and us the opportunity to render obedience from our hearts to the Lord?

5. What is one of the greatest challenges you are facing right now? How does it relate to the commands we have studied?

6. Which two or three of the commands studied in this series has been most challenging to you?

7. Is there an area of your heart or life that you need to submit to the Lord's control in obedience to His commands?

8. In what ways has the Lord given you victory and joy through steps of obedience you have taken in response to our study of God's commands?

Memory Verse
ROMANS 8:37–39

37 Nay, in all these things we are more than conquerors through him that loved us.

38 For I am persuaded, that neither death, nor life, nor angels, nor principalities, nor powers, nor things present, nor things to come,

39 Nor height, nor depth, nor any other creature, shall be able to separate us from the love of God, which is in Christ Jesus our Lord.

Striving Together
P u b l i c a t i o n s

For additional Christian
growth resources visit
www.strivingtogether.com